DINOSAURS

DINOSAURS

By Kathleen N. Daly

Pictures by
Tim and Greg Hildebrandt

gb Golden Press • New York
Western Publishing Company, Inc.
Racine, Wisconsin

Millions of years ago, our earth was the home of the dinosaurs. Among them were the biggest land animals that ever existed.

These huge creatures ruled the earth for a very long time. Then they disappeared, but nobody knows why. Only their bones and footprints, and some very old eggs, are left to tell us about them.

Scientists have put together dinosaur bones so we can see what those giant animals looked like.

RULERS OF THE LAND

When dinosaur bones were first found,
people thought they belonged to giant
lizards. The word "dinosaur" means
"terrible lizard," and the largest of these
beasts must have indeed seemed terrible to
smaller animals.

DINOSAURS THAT WALKED ON TWO LEGS

Some of the first dinosaurs were only about as big as a small dog. Over many, many years they grew bigger and bigger. As they grew, their looks and habits changed, too.

Dinosaurs that walked on two legs were able to move faster than those that walked on four legs. After a long time there were many dinosaurs with short front legs. They used them like arms, to grab food.

Some dinosaurs were meat-eaters. They attacked and ate other dinosaurs. ORNITHOLESTES (or′ni′tho′LES′-teez) was a meat-eater. This miniature dinosaur had a long, whiplike tail and grasping fingers. Its name means "bird stealer," and that's just what Ornitholestes was.

PLATEOSAURUS (plat'e'o'SORE'us) was the biggest
of the early dinosaurs. It was about 20 feet long,
with a small head and a whiplike tail. It ate only
plants, but smaller dinosaurs stayed out of the way of
this tall, swift-moving animal.

THE AGE OF GIANTS

BRACHIOSAURUS (brack'e'o'SORE'us), of the mighty arms and legs, was the largest dinosaur of all. It was more than 80 feet long and stood 40 feet tall. That's about as long as three city buses and as high as a four-story building. And Brachiosaurus weighed 100,000 pounds! Other creatures were lucky it ate only plants.

On land, this gentle giant was too heavy to run fast and escape from the meat-eaters. It spent most of its time in lakes. There the water held up its body and made it seem lighter.

Brachiosaurus' ear-shaped nostrils were at the top of its head so that it could breathe when most of its body was under water.

BRONTOSAURUS (bron'toe'SORE'us) was a giant among giants. Its name means "thunder lizard," and its footsteps must have sounded like thunder when it walked the earth. It was about 70 feet long and weighed more than 60,000 pounds.

Because this gentle plant-eater was so heavy, it hardly ever left the water. When it had to come to shore to lay its eggs, it often was attacked by the fierce Allosaurus.

ALLOSAURUS (al'lo'SORE'us), a meat-eating
dinosaur, had strong claws and terrible teeth.
It was only 35 feet long, but it could fight the
giant Brontosaurus that was twice its size.

DIPLODOCUS (dip′LOD′o′cus) was almost 90 feet long, and longer than any other dinosaur. But it was not as heavy as Brachiosaurus or Brontosaurus. It had a long, thin neck and a long, thin tail that it used like a whip.

When Diplodocus searched for food in the water, its neck looked like a sea serpent rising from the deep. Its teeth were not very strong, and it could take only small bites. So Diplodocus had to spend most of its time eating so as to get enough food for its huge body.

OVIRAPTOR (o'vee'RAP'tor) was a small
dinosaur that liked to eat the eggs of other
dinosaurs. Its name means "egg stealer."

THE NEW DINOSAURS

After a while, the really giant dinosaurs disappeared from the earth. Maybe it was because they needed to eat a great many plants to stay alive, and there just weren't enough to go around. Anyway, the giant dinosaurs died out. Along with them went many of the meat-eaters that needed those giant plant-eaters for food.

New kinds of dinosaurs came along. They were smaller and they couldn't move fast. But they were protected by tough, spiked coats of armor.

STEGOSAURUS (steg'o'SORE'us) had large, bony plates down its back and a thick tail that ended in sharp spikes. Stegosaurus was about 20 feet long, but its brain was only as big as a walnut.

ANKYLOSAUR (an'KY'lo'sore) had heavy plates of armor on its back. On each side were long spikes that continued down the tail. Ankylosaur used the knob at the end of its tail like a club.

GORGOSAURUS (gor'go'SORE'us) was a fierce meat-eating dinosaur that stood nearly 40 feet tall. It was a swift two-legged runner with long, powerful legs. The terrible jaws of Gorgosaurus were filled with sharp, daggerlike teeth that it used to grab and tear its food.

PROTOCERATOPS (pro'toe'SER'o'tops)
was a plant-eater that was only about six
feet long. It was often attacked by the big
meat-eaters. But Protoceratops was
protected by armor and a tough, bony frill
at the back of its head. It always put up
a good fight.

Another animal that lived in the
days of the dinosaur was the
RHAMPHORHYNCHUS (ram'
fo'RINK'us). It flew, but it was
a reptile, and not a bird. The
leathery skin that stretched
between its body and its arms
became its wings.

DUCKBILLS

Some dinosaurs lived along the shores of swamps. They had strange feet that were webbed like a duck's. With these huge feet, they could walk in the soft mud along the water's edge without sinking in.

TRACHODON (TRACK´o´don) was about 30 feet long. Its name means "rough tooth," and Trachodon had about 2,000 teeth in its duck-billed mouth.

IGUANODON (i'GWAN'o'don), or "lizard tooth," was smaller than Trachodon and had hands shaped like human hands. The thumb was a spiked claw. Iguanodon usually walked on two legs, balancing on its webbed feet and tail.

HORNED DINOSAURS

Many dinosaurs had horns on their heads and looked a little like large, fierce rhinoceroses. But these horned dinosaurs were peaceful plant-eaters. Their horns protected them from the sharp claws and powerful teeth of the meat-eaters.

STYRACOSAURUS (sty'rack'o'SORE'us), or "spike lizard," had a crown of six long horns on its head and another horn tilted up from its nose.

TRICERATOPS (try′SER′a′tops) was like an armored tank, with a long, bony collar and three sharp horns. This eight-ton plant-eater was about six feet tall and was feared by even the giant killer-dinosaurs.

TYRANNOSAURUS (tie´ ran´o´SORE´us) REX was the most terrible dinosaur that ever lived. This giant meat-eater was nearly 60 feet long and as tall as a two-story house.

Tyrannosaurus was a fierce hunter, and other dinosaurs feared its powerful jaws and long, sharp teeth. It was a "terrible lizard" indeed, and one of the last of the great dinosaurs.

PTERANODON (ter'AN'o'don) was a
large flying reptile. It had a wingspread of
over 20 feet.

TODAY'S REPTILES

Dinosaurs were reptiles. Although the dinosaurs have disappeared from the earth, many reptiles still live today. Like the dinosaurs, they lay eggs, keep cool in the water or in the shade, and bask in the sun to warm up again. Many lizards look just like miniature dinosaurs.

Crocodiles have scaly skins and rows of sharp teeth. Slithery, legless snakes remind us of the long necks of their ancestors.

The slow-moving turtles wear bony-plated armor, just as they did millions of years ago.